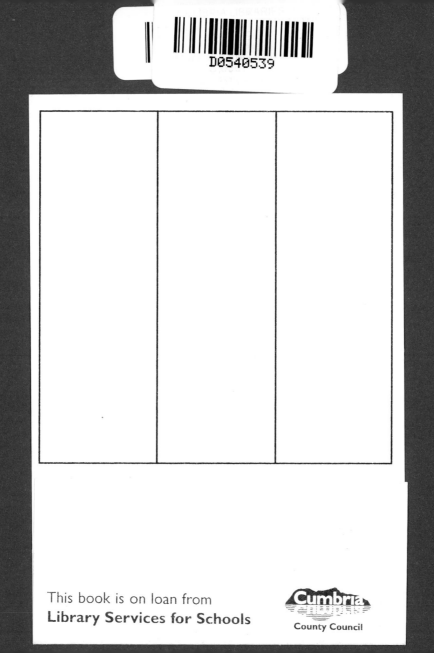

This book is on loan from
Library Services for Schools

Cumbria
County Council

Dinosaurs

Velociraptor

Daniel Nunn

www.heinemann.co.uk/library
Visit our website to find out more information about Heinemann Library books.

To order:
☎ Phone 44 (0) 1865 888066
   Send a fax to 44 (0) 1865 314091
📄 Visit the Heinemann Bookshop at www.heinemann.co.uk/library to browse our
💻 catalogue and order online.

First published in Great Britain by Heinemann Library, Halley Court, Jordan Hill, Oxford OX2 8EJ, part of Harcourt Education. Heinemann is a registered trademark of Harcourt Education Ltd.

Editorial: Daniel Nunn and Rachel Howells
Illustrations: James Field of Simon Girling and Associates
Design: Joanna Hinton-Malivoire
Picture research: Erica Newbery
Production: Duncan Gilbert

Printed and bound in China by South China Printing Co. Ltd.

10-digit ISBN 0 4311 8448 8
13-digit ISBN 978 0 4311 8448 7

11 10 09 08
10 9 8 7 6 5 4 3 2

British Library Cataloguing in Publication Data
Nunn, Daniel
Velociraptor. – (Dinosaurs)
567.9'12
A full catalogue record for this book is available from the British Library.

Acknowledgements
The publishers would like to thank the following for permission to reproduce photographs: Alamy p. 22 (blickwinkel); Corbis pp. 7 (Galen Rowell), 6, 21 (Louie Psihoyos), 12; Getty images pp. 18, 19 and 23 (Science Faction/Louie Psihoyos); Istock Photo pp. 6 and 16 (Steve Geer); Photographers direct p. 10 (Ottmar Bierwagen); Rex-features pp. 20 and 22 (Sipa Press).

Cover photograph of Velociraptor reproduced with permission of Istock Photo.

Every effort has been made to contact copyright holders of any material reproduced in this book. Any omissions will be rectified in subsequent printings if notice is given to the publishers.

Contents

The dinosaurs

Dinosaurs were reptiles.

Dinosaurs lived long ago.

Velociraptor was a dinosaur.
Velociraptor lived long ago.

Today there are no Velociraptor.

Velociraptor

Stegosaurus

Some dinosaurs were big.

But Velociraptor was small.

Velociraptor had a long tail.

Velociraptor could move very fast.

Velociraptor had sharp teeth.

claw

Velociraptor had long,
sharp claws.

Velociraptor attacked other dinosaurs.

Velociraptor ate other dinosaurs.

Velociraptor had good vision.

Velociraptor may have had feathers.

How do we know?

Scientists have found fossils
of Velociraptor.

Fossils are the bones of animals which have turned to rock.

fossil

Fossils show us the outline
of the dinosaur.

Fossils tell us what Velociraptor was like.

Fossil quiz

A

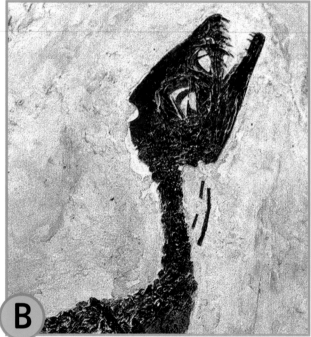

B

One of these fossils was Velociraptor.
Can you tell which one? Turn to page 24
to find out the answer.

Picture glossary

 **claw** hard, curved nails at the end of animals' feet

 **dinosaur** a reptile who lived millions of years ago

 **fossil** part of a dead plant or animal that has become hard like rock

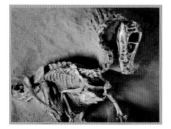 **reptile** a cold-blooded animal

Index

Answer to question on page 22
Fossil A was Diplodocus. Fossil B was Velociraptor.

Note to Parents and Teachers
Before reading
Talk to the children about dinosaurs. Do they know the names of any dinosaurs? What features did they have e.g. long neck, bony plates, sharp teeth? Has anyone seen a dinosaur fossil or model in a museum?

After reading
- Play 'I'm a Velociraptor' based on 'Grandma's Footsteps'. Stand with your back to the children. The children creep up towards you as you say you are one of the following herbivores: Diplodocus, Brachiosaurus, Triceratops. Then turn around and announce that you are a Velociraptor and run to catch one of the children.
- Give each child a piece of paper and tell them to use straws to make a dinosaur skeleton. When they are happy with the outline they should glue the straws to the paper.
- Look at a selection of non fiction books on dinosaurs e.g. *Dinosaur* (DK Eye Wonder)

Titles in the *Dinosaurs* series include:

Hardback   978-0431184500

Hardback   978-0431184517

Hardback   978-0431184494

Hardback   978-0431184470

Hardback   978-0431184463

Hardback   978-0431184487

Find out about other titles from Heinemann Library on our website www.heinemann.co.uk/library